BRIAN the BRAIN
MIND...SET...GO!

Copyright © 2024 by Jennifer Misener

All rights reserved. No part of this book may be reproduced or used in any manner without written permission of the copyright owner except for the use of quotations in a book review. For more information, address:
authorjennymouse@gmail.com

First paperback edition November 2024

ISBN 978-1-7774943-5-3 (paperback)
ISBN 978-1-7774943-6-0 (ebook)

jennymouse.com

About the Author

Jenny Mouse is the mom of three science-loving kids! She lives in beautiful Ontario, Canada, and loves passing the long winters creating stories and doing experiments. She's passionate about brain health and wants to make sure everyone realizes how important it is to understand and take care of your brain.

For Felix, Lucy, and Vincent.

With a special thanks
to my husband Nathan,
and my good friend
Sarah
for all the help and support.

About the Illustrator

John Peter Meiring is an award-winning freelance designer and animator based in London, UK. As a freelance designer, he specialises in all areas of graphic design and illustration from branding, and social media content to brand world illustration. He has worked as a freelance graphic designer for over 10 years, helping brands of all shapes and sizes stand out with bold and memorable designs and illustrations.

About the Subject Matter Expert

Robin Katz holds a doctorate in Occupational Therapy from Boston University (2012) and a Master's of Social Work from Wurzweiler School of Social Work (2006). She teaches her clients about the brain as part of her practice.

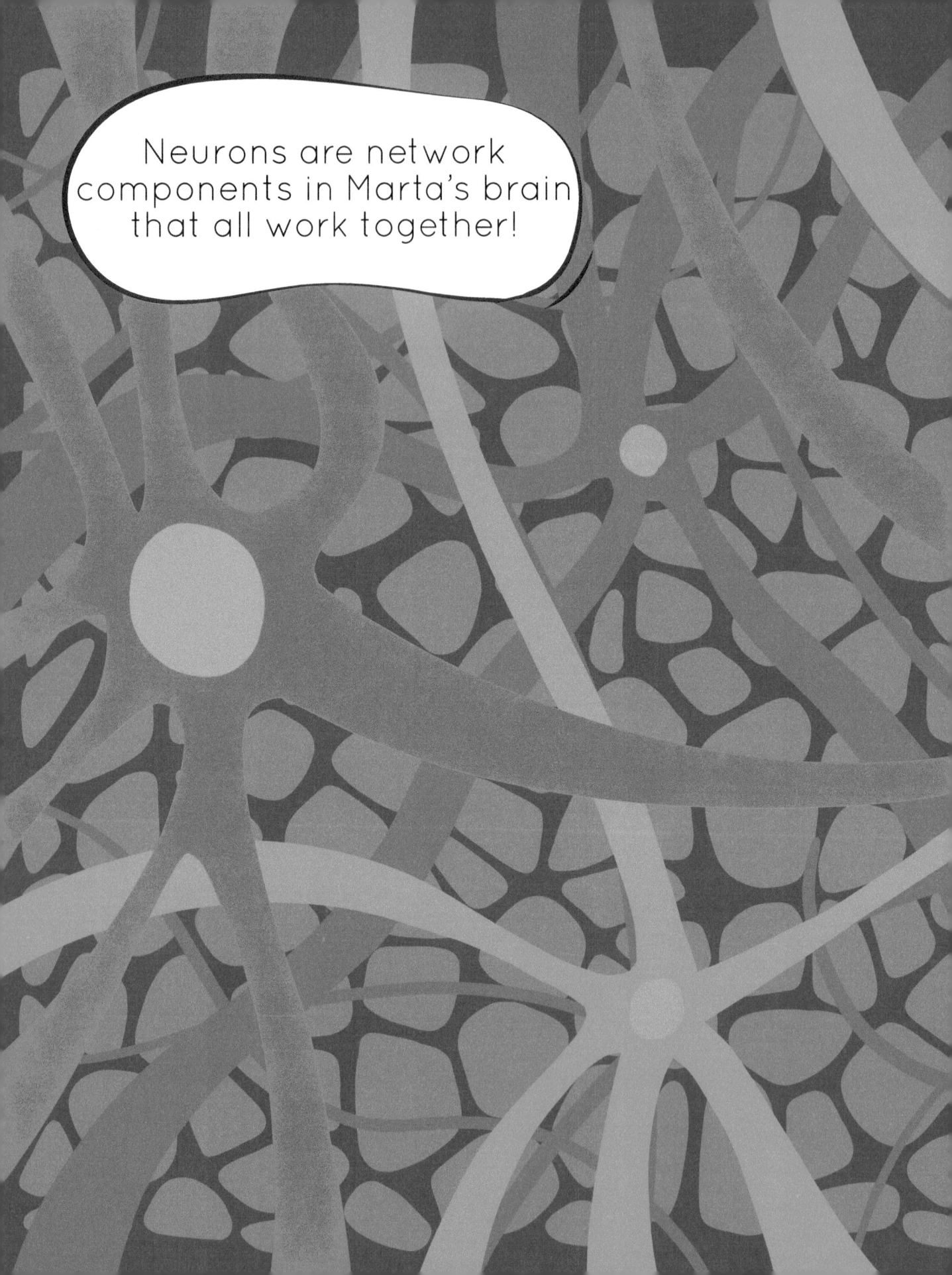

Pretty soon, the moment comes when Marta can do the job!

Growth Mindset Lessons From Today's Story:

1. Say "I can't YET" when you get frustrated. You can do anything if you keep on trying!

2. Mistakes help your brain learn.

3. If you find something hard, try doing it a different way.

4. You are never too old to learn something new.

5. 'Practice makes progress!'

Next time, join us again to learn more about the workings of your brain.

You'll also be giving your brain some good exercise!

www.ingramcontent.com/pod-product-compliance
Lightning Source LLC
Chambersburg PA
CBHW041526070526
44585CB00002B/94